RING~A~RING
O' ROSES

Dedicated to:
Abigail and Philip,
Ian Spencer,
and Joanne Michelle

Special thanks to Vida Williams for
designing this book with care and imagination

J.T.

VIKING

Published by the Penguin Group
Penguin Books Ltd, 27 Wrights Lane, London W8 5TZ, England
Penguin Putnam Inc., 345 Hudson Street, New York, New York 10014, USA
Penguin Books Australia Ltd, Ringwood, Victoria, Australia
Penguin Books Canada Ltd, 10 Alcorn Avenue, Toronto, Ontario, Canada M4V 3B2
Penguin Books (NZ) Ltd, 182–190 Wairau Road, Auckland 10, New Zealand

Penguin Books Ltd, Registered Offices: Harmondsworth, Middlesex, England

First published 1998
1 3 5 7 9 10 8 6 4 2

Set in monotype baskerville

Made and printed in Italy by L.E.G.O.

British Library Cataloguing in Publication Data
A CIP catalogue record for this book is available from the British Library

ISBN 0–670–87302–0

This edition produced for
The Book People Ltd, Hall Wood Avenue,
Haydock, St Helens WA11 9UL

RING~A~RING
O' ROSES

A Collection of Nursery Rhymes and Stories

Illustrated by Justin Todd

TED SMART

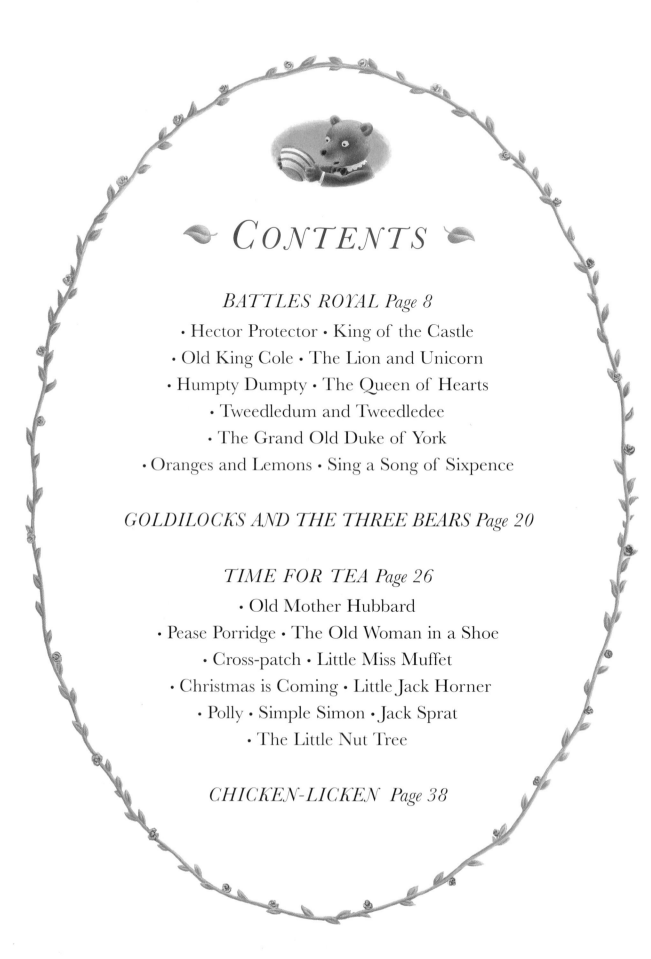

Contents

BATTLES ROYAL Page 8

• Hector Protector • King of the Castle
• Old King Cole • The Lion and Unicorn
• Humpty Dumpty • The Queen of Hearts
• Tweedledum and Tweedledee
• The Grand Old Duke of York
• Oranges and Lemons • Sing a Song of Sixpence

GOLDILOCKS AND THE THREE BEARS Page 20

TIME FOR TEA Page 26
• Old Mother Hubbard
• Pease Porridge • The Old Woman in a Shoe
• Cross-patch • Little Miss Muffet
• Christmas is Coming • Little Jack Horner
• Polly • Simple Simon • Jack Sprat
• The Little Nut Tree

CHICKEN-LICKEN Page 38

CREATURES, GREAT AND SMALL Page 44

· Little Bo-peep · My Black Hen · To the Magpie
· The Mischievous Raven · Mary's Lamb
· Ride a Cock-horse · Yankee Doodle
· Hey Diddle, Diddle · Robin and Jenny · The Owl

THE GINGERBREAD MAN Page 54

BOYS AND GIRLS Page 60

· Georgie Porgie · Lavender's Blue
· Contrary Mary · Boys and Girls · The Little Girl
· Roses are Red · Curly Locks · Bobby Shaftoe · Sally · Tom
· The Milk Maid · Polly Flinders · Jack and Jill

LITTLE RED RIDING-HOOD Page 72

RAIN AND SHINE Page 78

· Here We Go Round the Mulberry Bush
· Doctor Foster · The North Wind
· It's Raining · To the Rain · Daffy-down-dilly
· Spring · Ipsey Wipsey Spider

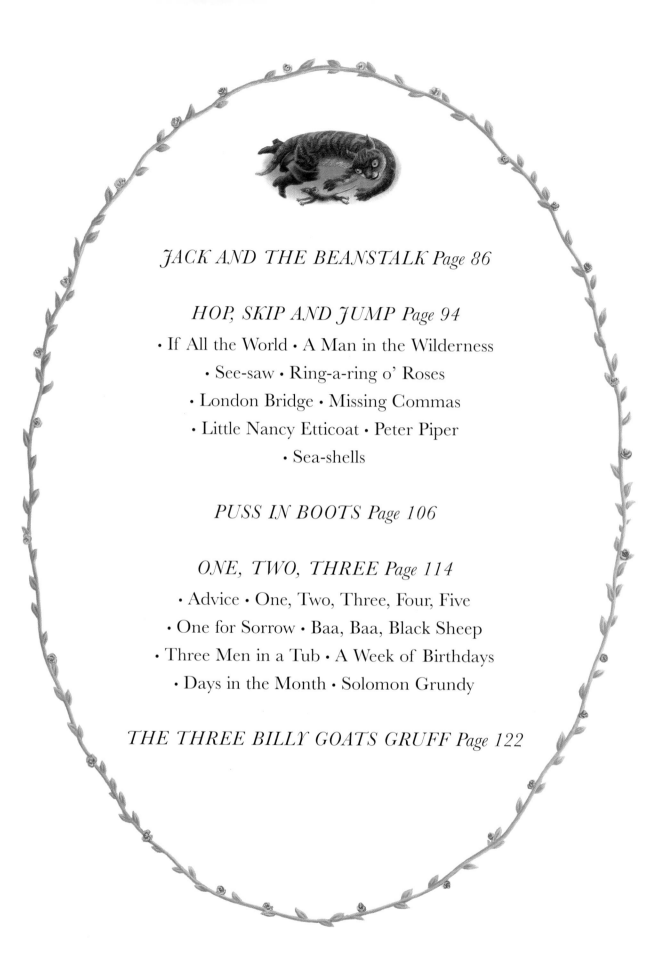

JACK AND THE BEANSTALK Page 86

HOP, SKIP AND JUMP Page 94
· If All the World · A Man in the Wilderness
· See-saw · Ring-a-ring o' Roses
· London Bridge · Missing Commas
· Little Nancy Etticoat · Peter Piper
· Sea-shells

PUSS IN BOOTS Page 106

ONE, TWO, THREE Page 114
· Advice · One, Two, Three, Four, Five
· One for Sorrow · Baa, Baa, Black Sheep
· Three Men in a Tub · A Week of Birthdays
· Days in the Month · Solomon Grundy

THE THREE BILLY GOATS GRUFF Page 122

CAT AND MOUSE *Page 128*

• Hickory, Dickory, Dock • The Squirrel
• The Crooked Man • Three Blind Mice
• Hoddley, Poddley • Six Little Mice
• The Three Little Kittens
• Ding, Dong, Bell • The Beggars
• Three Young Rats • Pussy Cat

THE THREE LITTLE PIGS *Page 140*

STAR LIGHT, STAR BRIGHT *Page 146*

• Going to Bed • Wee Willie Winkie
• Bedtime • Diddle, Diddle, Dumpling
• Goosey Gander • Boy Blue
• Hush-a-bye • The Old Woman
• The Mocking Bird • Star Light
• Boys and Girls Come Out to Play

BATTLES ROYAL

Hector Protector
was dressed all in green;
Hector Protector
was sent to the Queen.
The Queen did not like him,
No more did the King;
So Hector Protector
was sent back again.

I'm the KING of the castle,

GET DOWN you dirty rascal.

Old King Cole
Was a MERRY old soul,
And a merry old soul was he;
He called for his pipe,
And he called for his bowl,
And he called for his FIDDLERS three.

Every FIDDLER he had a fiddle,
And a very fine fiddle had he;
Oh, there's none so rare
As can compare
With King Cole and his FIDDLERS three.

The lion and the unicorn
Were fighting for the crown;
The lion beat the unicorn
    All around the town.

        Some gave them white bread,
           And some gave them brown;
        Some gave them plum cake
           And drummed them out of town.

Humpty Dumpty sat on a wall,
Humpty Dumpty had a great fall;
All the King's horses and all the King's men
Couldn't put Humpty together again.

The Queen of Hearts
She made some tarts,
All on a summer's day;
The Knave of Hearts
He stole those tarts,
And took them clean away.

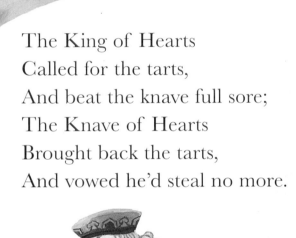

The King of Hearts
Called for the tarts,
And beat the knave full sore;
The Knave of Hearts
Brought back the tarts,
And vowed he'd steal no more.

Tweedledum and Tweedledee
　　Agreed to have a battle,
For Tweedledum said Tweedledee
　　Had spoiled his nice new rattle.

Just then flew by a monstrous crow
　　As black as a tar-barrel,
Which frightened both the heroes so,
　　They quite forgot their quarrel.

Oh, the grand old
Duke of York,

He had ten thousand men;

He marched them up to the top of the hill,

And he marched them down again.

And when they were up, they were up,

And when they were down, they were down,

And when they were only half way up,

They were neither up nor down.

Bull's eyes and targets,
Say the bells of St Marg'ret's.

Brickbats and tiles,
Say the bells of St Giles'.

Oranges and lemons,
Say the bells of St Clement's.

Pancakes and fritters,
Say the bells of St Peter's.

Two sticks and an apple,
Say the bells at Whitechapel.

Old Father Baldpate,
Say the slow bells at Aldgate.

Maids in white aprons,
Say the bells at St Catherine's.

Pokers and tongs,
Say the bells at St John's.

Kettles and pans,
Say the bells at St Anne's.

You owe me five farthings,
Say the bells of St Martin's.

When will you pay me?
Say the bells at Old Bailey.

When I grow rich,
Say the bells at Shoreditch.

Pray, when will that be?
Say the bells at Stepney.

I'm sure I don't know,
Says the great bell at Bow.

Here comes a candle
to light you to bed,
Here comes a chopper
to chop off your head.

Sing a song of sixpence,
A pocket full of rye;
Four and twenty blackbirds,
Baked in a pie.

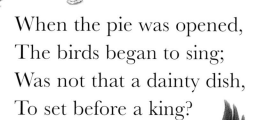

When the pie was opened,
The birds began to sing;
Was not that a dainty dish,
To set before a king?

The king was in his counting-house,
Counting out his money;
The queen was in the parlour,
Eating bread and honey.

The maid was in the garden,
Hanging out her clothes,
When down came a blackbird
And pecked off her nose.

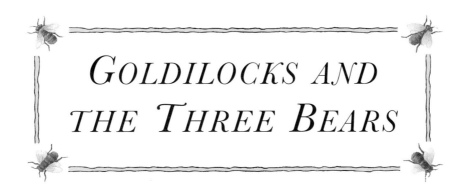

GOLDILOCKS AND THE THREE BEARS

Once upon a time there were three bears who lived in a cottage in a wood.

One of the bears was a GREAT BIG BEAR.

One was a MIDDLE-SIZED BEAR.

And one was a TINY WEE BEAR.

One day the three bears made the porridge for their breakfast and went for a walk in the wood while it was cooling.

The great big bear had a great big bowl for his porridge.

The middle-sized bear had a middle-sized bowl for her porridge.

And the tiny wee bear had a tiny wee bowl for his porridge.

While the bears were out a pretty little girl called Goldilocks, who lived in a house near the wood, came to their cottage. She saw the door was open and so she peeped inside.

There she saw a table with the three bowls of porridge on it.

Goldilocks could see no one about and she was feeling

very hungry so she went into the cottage.

First she tasted the porridge in the great big bowl, with a great big spoon, but it was far too hot, and it burned her tongue.

Then she tasted the porridge in the middle-sized bowl with a middle-sized spoon, but it was still too hot and she did not like it.

And last she tasted the porridge in the tiny wee bowl, with a tiny wee spoon, and it was just right, neither too hot nor too cold, so she ate it all up, every drop.

Goldilocks felt tired now, so she looked round and then she saw three chairs.

One was a great big chair.

One was a middle-sized chair.

And one was a tiny wee chair.

First she sat in the great big chair, but it was too hard for her.

Then she sat in the middle-sized chair, but it was too soft for her.

And last she sat in the tiny wee chair, and it was just right, neither too hard nor too soft, but very comfortable. So she went on sitting on it till suddenly the bottom of the chair fell out and she found herself sitting on the floor. The tiny wee chair was not made for anyone as big as Goldilocks.

Goldilocks felt very sleepy now, so she looked round the room and saw some steep stairs. 'I'll go upstairs now,' she thought.

So she went upstairs and into a little bedroom.

There she saw three beds.

One was a great big bed.

One was a middle-sized bed.

And one was a tiny wee bed.

First she lay down on the great big bed, but it was too high at the head for her.

Then she lay down on the middle-sized bed, but it was too low at the foot for her.

And last she lay down on the tiny wee bed, and it was just right, neither too high at the head nor too low at the foot. So she went on lying on it till she fell fast asleep.

Just then the three bears came home from their walk in the wood, ready for their breakfast.

First the great big bear saw his great big spoon standing in his porridge in his great big bowl.

'SOMEONE HAS BEEN TASTING MY PORRIDGE,' he roared in his great gruff voice.

Then the middle-sized bear saw her middle-sized spoon standing in her middle-sized bowl.

'SOMEONE HAS BEEN TASTING MY PORRIDGE,' she growled in her middle-sized voice.

And last the tiny wee bear saw his tiny wee spoon standing in his empty tiny wee bowl.

'SOMEONE HAS BEEN TASTING MY PORRIDGE,' he squeaked in his tiny wee voice, 'AND HAS EATEN IT ALL UP.'

Now the great big bear saw that the great big cushion in his great big chair was crumpled.

'SOMEONE HAS BEEN SITTING IN MY CHAIR,' he roared in his great gruff voice.

Then the middle-sized bear saw that the middle-sized cushion in her middle-sized chair was crumpled.

'SOMEONE HAS BEEN SITTING IN MY CHAIR,' she growled in her middle-sized voice.

And last the tiny wee bear saw that the tiny wee cushion of his tiny wee chair was lying on the floor, and that the chair was broken.

'SOMEONE HAS BEEN SITTING ON MY CHAIR,' he squeaked in his tiny wee voice, 'AND HAS SAT THE BOTTOM OUT OF IT.'

The three bears looked all round but they could see nobody.

So they went up the steep stairs into their bedroom.

First the great big bear saw that the bedclothes on his great big bed were untidy.

'SOMEONE HAS BEEN LYING ON MY BED,' he roared in his great gruff voice.

Then the middle-sized bear saw that the bedclothes on her middle-sized bed were untidy.

'SOMEONE HAS BEEN LYING ON MY BED,' she growled in her middle-sized voice.

And last the tiny wee bear saw that the bedclothes on his tiny wee bed were covering a queer little hump.

'SOMEONE HAS BEEN LYING ON MY BED,' he squeaked in his tiny wee voice, 'AND HERE SHE IS!'

Then Goldilocks awoke and she was very frightened to see the three bears.

She jumped out of the tiny wee bed and ran down the stairs.

When the three bears got downstairs she had run out of the door and when they got to the door she was a long way off. And though they ran and ran, they did not catch her for she had run through the wood and was safe with her mother and father at home.

So the three bears went back to their cottage.

TIME FOR TEA

Old Mother Hubbard
Went to the cupboard,
To fetch her poor dog a bone;
But when she got there
The cupboard was bare
And so the poor dog had none.

Pease porridge HOT,
Pease porridge COLD,
Pease porridge in the pot
Nine days old.

Some like it HOT,
Some like it COLD,
Some like it in the pot
Nine days old.

There was an old woman
who lived in a shoe,
She had so many children
she didn't know what to do;
She gave them some broth
without any bread;
She whipped them all soundly
and sent them to bed.

Cross-patch,
Draw the latch,
Sit by the fire and spin;
Take a cup,
And drink it up,
Then call your neighbours in.

Little Miss Muffet
Sat on a tuffet,
Eating her curds and whey;

There came a big spider,

Who sat down beside her

And frightened Miss Muffet away.

Christmas is coming,
The geese are getting fat,
Please to put a penny
In the old man's hat.
If you haven't got a penny,
A ha'penny will do;
If you haven't got a ha'penny,
Then God bless you!

Little Jack Horner
Sat in the corner,
Eating his Christmas pie;
He put in his thumb,
And pulled out a plum,
And said,
What a good boy am I!

Polly put the kettle **on**,
Polly put the kettle **on**,
Polly put the kettle **on**,
We'll all have tea.

Sukey take it **off** again,
Sukey take it **off** again,
Sukey take it **off** again,
They've all gone away.

Simple Simon met a pieman
   Going to the fair;
Says Simple Simon to the pieman,
   Let me taste your ware.

     Say the pieman to Simple Simon,
       Show me first your penny;
     Says Simple Simon to the pieman,
       Indeed I have not any.

Simple Simon went a-fishing,
   For to catch a whale;
All the water he had got
   Was in his mother's pail.

     Simple Simon went a-hunting,
       For to catch a hare;
     He rode a goat about the streets,
       But couldn't find one there.

He went to catch a dickey bird,
   And thought he could not fail,
Because he'd got a little salt,
   To put upon its tail.

He went to shoot a wild duck,
    But wild duck flew away;
Says Simon, I can't hit him,
    Because he will not stay.

He went to ride a spotted cow,
    That had a little calf;
She threw him down upon the ground,
    Which made the people laugh.

Once Simon made a great snowball,
    And brought it in to roast;
He laid it down before the fire,
    And soon the ball was lost.

He went to try if cherries ripe
    Did grow upon a thistle;
He pricked his finger very much
    Which made poor Simon whistle.

He went for water in a sieve,
    But soon it all ran through;
And now poor Simple Simon
    Bids you all adieu.

Jack
Sprat
could
eat
no
fat,
His
wife
could
eat
no
lean,
And
so
between
them
both,
you
see,
They
licked
the
platter
clean.

I had a little nut tree,
Nothing would it bear
But a silver nutmeg
And a golden pear;
The king of Spain's daughter
Came to visit me,
And all for the sake
of my little nut tree.

CHICKEN-LICKEN

As Chicken-licken was at the wood one day, an acorn fell from a tree on his poor bald head.

'Gracious me,' thought Chicken-licken, 'the sky is falling! I must go and tell the King.'

So he turned back and he met Hen-len. 'Well, Hen-len, where are you going?' he asked. 'I'm going to the wood,' said she. So Chicken-licken said, 'Oh, Hen-len, don't go, for I was there and the sky fell on my poor bald head, and I'm going to tell the King.'

'May I come with you?' said Hen-len. 'Certainly,' said Chicken-licken. So Hen-len turned back with Chicken-licken, and they went together to tell the King the sky was falling.

And as they went, they met Cock-lock. 'Well, Cock-lock, where are you going?' asked Hen-len. 'I'm going to the wood,' said he. So Hen-len said, 'Oh Cock-lock, don't go, for Chicken-licken was there and the sky fell on his poor bald head, and we're going to tell the King.'

'May I come with you?' said Cock-lock. 'Certainly,' said Chicken-licken and Hen-len. So Cock-lock turned back with Chicken-licken and Hen-len and they all three went to tell the King the sky was falling.

And as they went they met Duck-luck. 'Well, Duck-luck, where are you going?' asked Cock-lock. 'I'm going to the wood,' said she. So Cock-lock said, 'Oh Duck-luck, don't go, for Chicken-licken was there, and the sky fell on his poor bald head, and we're going to tell the King.'

'May I come with you?' said Duck-luck. 'Certainly,' said Chicken-licken and Hen-len and Cock-lock. So Duck-luck turned back with Chicken-licken and Hen-len and Cock-lock, and they all four went to tell the King the sky was falling.

And as they went they met Drake-lake. 'Well, Drake-lake, where are you going?' asked Duck-luck. 'I'm going to the wood,' said he. So Duck-luck said, 'Oh Drake-lake, don't go, for Chicken-licken was there and the sky fell on

his poor bald head and we're going to tell the King.'

'May I come with you?' said Drake-lake. 'Certainly,' said Chicken-licken and Hen-len and Cock-lock and Duck-luck. So Drake-lake turned back with Chicken-licken, and Hen-len and Cock-lock and Duck-luck, and they all five went to tell the King the sky was falling.

And as they went they met Goose-loose. 'Well, Goose-loose, where are you going?' asked Drake-lake. 'I'm going to the wood,' said she. So Drake-lake said, 'Oh Goose-loose, don't go, for Chicken-licken was there and the sky fell on his poor bald head and we're going to tell the King.'

'May I come with you?' said Goose-loose. 'Certainly,' said Chicken-licken and Hen-len and Cock-lock and Duck-luck and Drake-lake. So Goose-loose turned back with Chicken-licken and Hen-len and Cock-lock and

Duck-luck and Drake-lake and they all six went to tell the King the sky was falling.

And as they went they met Gander-lander. 'Well, Gander-lander, where are you going?' asked Goose-loose. 'I'm going to the wood,' said he. So Goose-loose said, 'Oh Gander-lander, don't go, for Chicken-licken was there and the sky fell on his poor bald head and we're going to tell the King.'

'May I come with you?' said Gander-lander. 'Certainly,' said Chicken-licken and Hen-len and Cock-lock and Duck-luck and Drake-lake and Goose-loose. So Gander-lander turned back with Chicken-licken and Hen-len and Cock-lock and Duck-luck and Drake-lake and Goose-loose, and they all seven went to tell the King the sky was falling.

And as they went they met Turkey-lurkey. 'Well, Turkey-lurkey, where are you going?' asked Gander-lander. 'I'm going to the wood,' said he. So Gander-lander said, 'Oh Turkey-lurkey, don't go for Chicken-licken was there and the sky fell on his poor bald head and we're going to tell the King.'

'May I come with you?' said Turkey-lurkey. 'Certainly,' said Chicken-licken and Hen-len and Cock-lock and Duck-luck and Drake-lake and Goose-loose and Gander-lander. So Turkey-lurkey turned back with Chicken-licken and Hen-len and Cock-lock and Duck-luck and Drake-lake and Goose-loose and Gander-lander and they all eight went to tell the King the sky was falling.

And as they went they met Fox-lox. And Fox-lox said, 'Where are you going?' and they said, 'Chicken-licken went to the wood, and the sky fell on his poor bald head, and we're going to tell the King.'

Then Fox-lox said: 'Come with me and I will show you the way.' So they went with him until they came to a dark and narrow hole. 'This is the way,' said Fox-lox. So in they went one after the other, but it was not the way to the King, it was Fox-lox's own hole, and he and his young ones soon ate up poor Chicken-licken, Hen-len, Cock-lock, Duck-luck, Drake-lake, Goose-loose, Gander-lander and Turkey-lurkey.

And so they never saw the King to tell him that the sky was falling.

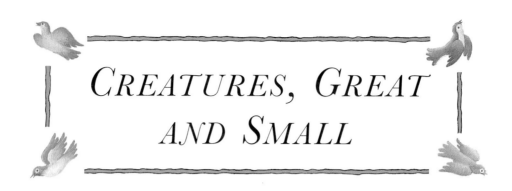

CREATURES, GREAT AND SMALL

Little Bo-peep has lost her sheep,
And doesn't know where to find them;
Leave them alone, and they'll come home,
Bringing their tails behind them.

Little Bo-peep fell fast asleep,
And dreamt she heard them bleating;
But when she awoke, she found it a joke,
For they were still a-fleeting.

Then up she took her little crook,
Determined for to find them;
She found them indeed, but it made her heart bleed
For they'd left their tails behind them.

It happened one day, as Bo-peep did stray
Into a meadow hard by,
There she spied their tails side by side,
All hung on a tree to dry.

She heaved a sigh, and wiped her eye,
And over the hillocks went rambling,
And tried what she could, as a shepherdess should,
To tack again each to its lambkin.

Hickety, Pickety
my black hen,
She lays eggs for gentlemen;
Gentlemen come every day
To see what my black hen doth lay.

Magpie, magpie, flutter and flee,

Turn up your tail and good luck come to me.

A farmer went trotting upon his grey mare,
B u m p e t y, b u m p e t y, b u m p!
With his daughter behind him so rosy and fair,
L u m p e t y, l u m p e t y, l u m p!

A raven cried, Croak! and they all tumbled down,
B u m p e t y, b u m p e t y, b u m p!
The mare broke her knees and the farmer his crown,
L u m p e t y, l u m p e t y, l u m p!

The mischievous raven flew laughing away,
B u m p e t y, b u m p e t y, b u m p!
And vowed he would serve them the same the next day,
L u m p e t y, l u m p e t y, l u m p!

Mary had a little lamb
Its fleece was white as snow;
And everywhere that Mary went
The lamb was sure to go.

It followed her to school one day,
That was against the rule;
It made the children laugh and play
To see a lamb at school.

And so the teacher turned it out,
But still it lingered near,
And waited patiently about
Till Mary did appear.

Why does the lamb love Mary so?
The eager children cry;
Why, Mary loves the lamb, you know,
The teacher did reply.

Ride a cock-horse
to Banbury Cross,
To see a fine lady
upon a white horse;
Rings on her fingers
and bells on her toes,
And she shall have music
wherever she goes.

Yankee Doodle came to town,
Riding on a pony;
He stuck a feather in his cap
And called it macaroni.

Hey diddle, diddle,
The cat and the fiddle,
The cow jumped over the moon;
The little dog laughed to see such sport,
And the dish ran away with the spoon.

Jenny Wren fell sick
     Upon a merry time,
In came Robin Redbreast
     And brought her sops and wine.
Eat well of the sop, Jenny,
     Drink well of the wine,
Thank you, Robin, kindly,
     You shall be mine.

Jenny Wren got well,
     And stood upon her feet;
And told Robin plainly,
     She loved him not a bit.
Robin he got angry,
     And hopped upon a twig,
Saying, Out upon you, fie upon you,
     Bold faced jig!

A wise old
owl sat in an oak,
The more he heard
the less he spoke;
The less he spoke
the more he heard.
Why aren't we all
like that wise old bird?

THE GINGERBREAD MAN

An old woman was baking cakes in her oven, and she thought it would be a good idea to make a little gingerbread man. So she shaped the dough into a little man, and put currants for his eyes and nose and mouth and the buttons on his jacket, and when he was finished she put him in the oven with the other cakes to bake.

After a while she heard a little voice from the oven calling out:

'Let me out! Open the door and let me out!'

She was very surprised, so she opened the oven door to see what it was. Out jumped the little gingerbread man and away he ran out of the kitchen through the door and into the garden.

'Quick,' called the old woman to her husband, 'catch him before he gets away!' The old man and the old woman ran as hard as they could, but they couldn't catch the little gingerbread man.

On and on ran the little gingerbread man, out of the garden and into the road, and soon he met two men who were digging a well.

'Where are you going?' they asked.

'Aha!' said the gingerbread man. 'I've run away from a

little old woman and a little old man and I can run away from you too, I can.

Run, run, as fast as you can,
You can't catch me, I'm the gingerbread man!'

'Oh can't we!' they said, and they ran after him as fast as they could, but they couldn't catch him and soon had to stop to rest.

On and on ran the little gingerbread man and soon he met two men who were digging a ditch.

'Where are you going?' they asked.

'Aha!' said the gingerbread man. 'I've run away from a little old woman and a little old man, and two well-diggers and I can run away from you too, I can.

Run, run, as fast as you can,

You can't catch me, I'm the gingerbread man!'

'Oh can't we!' they said, and they ran after him as fast as they could, but they couldn't catch him and soon had to stop to rest.

On and on ran the little gingerbread man and soon he met a bear.

'Where are you going?' asked the bear.

'Aha!' said the gingerbread man. 'I've run away from a little old woman, and a little old man, and two well-diggers and two ditch-diggers and I can run away from you too, I can.

Run, run, as fast as you can,

You can't catch me, I'm the gingerbread man!'

'Oh can't I!' said the bear, and he ran after him as fast as he could, but he couldn't catch him, and soon had to stop to rest.

On and on ran the little gingerbread man, and soon he met a wolf.

'Where are you going?' asked the wolf.

'Aha!' said the gingerbread man. 'I've run away from a little old woman and a little old man and two well-diggers and two ditch-diggers and a bear, and I can run away from you too, I can.

Run, run, as fast as you can,

You can't catch me, I'm the gingerbread man!'

'Oh can't I!' said the wolf, and he ran after him as fast as he could, but he couldn't catch him, and soon had to stop to rest.

On and on ran the little gingerbread man, until he came to a river. And then he had to stop.

Along came a fox. 'Where are you going?' he said.

'Aha!' said the gingerbread man. 'I've run away from a little old woman, and a little old man, and two well-diggers, and two ditch-diggers, and a bear and a wolf, and I can run away from you too, I can.

Run, run, as fast as you can,

You can't catch me, I'm the gingerbread man!'

But the fox said, 'I don't want to catch you. Jump on my back and I'll carry you across the river.'

So the little gingerbread man jumped up on the fox's back. Into the water went the fox and the water came up nearly over his back.

'You'd better climb on to my shoulders,' said the fox. 'The water's getting higher.'

So the little gingerbread man climbed up on to the fox's shoulders, but the water got higher still and the fox said:

'You'd better climb on to the top of my head now, in case you get wet.'

So the little gingerbread man climbed up on to the top of the fox's head, but the water got higher still and the fox said: 'You'd better climb on to my nose – I can keep it out of the water easiest.'

So the little gingerbread man climbed up on to the fox's nose, but as soon as they got to the other side of the river the fox tossed his head into the air, up went the little gingerbread man and down he came right into the fox's mouth. And the fox crunched him all up in an instant!

BOYS AND GIRLS

Georgie Porgie,
Pudding and pie,
Kissed the girls
And made them cry;
When the boys
Came out to play,
Georgie Porgie ran away.

Lavender's blue,
dilly, dilly.
Lavender's green.
When I am king,
dilly, dilly,
You shall be queen.

Call up your men,
dilly, dilly.
Set them to work.
Some to the plough,
dilly, dilly.
Some to the cart.

Some to make hay,
dilly, dilly.
Some to thresh corn.
While you and I,
dilly, dilly.
Keep ourselves warm.

Mary, Mary, quite contrary,
How does your garden grow?
With silver bells and cockle shells,
And pretty maids all in a row.

What are little boys
made of, made of?
What are little boys
made of?
Frogs
and snails
And
puppy-dogs'
tails,

That's what little
boys are made of.

What are little girls
made of, made of?
What are little girls
made of?
Sugar
and spice
And
all things
nice,

That's what little
girls are made of.

There was a little
girl, and she had
a little curl, right
in the middle
of her forehead.
When she was
good she was
very, very
good, but
when she
was bad
she was
horrid.

Roses are red,
Violets are blue,
Honey is sweet
And so are you.

Curly locks, Curly locks,
Wilt thou be mine?
Thou shalt not wash dishes
Nor yet feed the swine;
But sit on a cushion
And sew a fine seam,
And feed upon strawberries,
Sugar and cream.

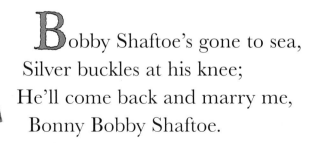

Bobby Shaftoe's gone to sea,
Silver buckles at his knee;
He'll come back and marry me,
    Bonny Bobby Shaftoe.

Bobby Shaftoe's bright and fair,
    Combing down his yellow hair,
    He's my ain for evermair,
    Bonny Bobby Shaftoe.

Bobby Shaftoe's tall and slim,
He's always dressed so neat and trim,
The ladies they all keek at him,
    Bonny Bobby Shaftoe.

Bobby Shaftoe's getten a bairn
    For to dandle in his arm;
    In his arm and on his knee,
    Bobby Shaftoe loves me.

Sally go round the sun, Sally go round the moon, Sally go round the chimney-pots on a Saturday afternoon.

Tom, Tom,
the piper's son,
Stole a pig
and away he run;
The pig was eat,
And Tom was beat,
And Tom went howling
down the street.

Where are you going to, my pretty maid?
I'm going a-milking, sir, she said,
Sir, she said, sir, she said,
I'm going a-milking, sir, she said.

May I go with you, my pretty maid?
You're kindly welcome, sir, she said,
Sir, she said, sir, she said,
You're kindly welcome, sir, she said.

Say, will you marry me, my pretty maid?
Yes, if you please, kind sir, she said,
Sir, she said, sir, she said,
Yes, if you please, kind sir, she said.

What is your father, my pretty maid?
My father's a farmer, sir, she said,
Sir, she said, sir, she said,
My father's a farmer, sir, she said.

What is your fortune, my pretty maid?
My face is my fortune, sir, she said,
Sir, she said, sir, she said,
My face is my fortune, sir, she said.

Then I can't marry you, my pretty maid.
Nobody asked you, sir, she said,
Sir, she said, sir, she said,
Nobody asked you, sir, she said.

Little Polly Flinders sat among the cinders,
Warming her pretty little toes;
Her mother came and caught her,
And whipped her little daughter
For spoiling her nice new clothes.

Jack and Jill
Went up the hill,
To fetch a pail of water;
Jack fell down,
And broke his crown,
And Jill came tumbling after.

Then up Jack got,
And home did trot,
As fast as he could caper;
And went to bed
To mend his head
With vinegar and brown paper.

When Jill came in,
How she did grin
To see Jack's paper plaster;
Her mother, vexed,
Did whip her next,
For laughing at Jack's disaster.

Now Jack did laugh
And Jill did cry,
But her tears did soon abate;
Then Jill did say,
That they should play
At see-saw across the gate.

LITTLE RED RIDING-HOOD

In a cottage near a wood there once lived a little girl. Her grandmother, who lived at the other side of the wood, had made her a beautiful little red cloak with a hood, which suited her so well that everyone called her Little Red Riding-Hood.

One day Little Red Riding-Hood's mother said:

'My dear, your granny has not been well, so I want you to go and see if she is better, and take her this basket I have packed with cakes, cream and eggs, and a little pot of butter. Keep on the road to Granny's cottage and come straight home again, and don't talk to anybody you don't know on the way. Do you understand?'

Little Red Riding-Hood was happy to think of going to see her grandmother. So she put on her cloak, took the basket on her arm and started off at once. But she did not do as her mother had told her. She did not keep to the road but went through the wood because it was prettier. And in the wood she met a wolf.

Now the wolf was hungry and he wanted to eat her, but he was afraid because some woodcutters were working near by in the wood. So he said:

'Good morning! Where are you going, my dear?'

Little Red Riding-Hood, not knowing how dangerous it was to talk to a wolf, and forgetting what her mother had told her, replied:

'I'm going to see my grandmother to take her this basket of cakes and cream and eggs and a little pot of butter.'

'Where does she live?' asked the wolf.

'In a cottage at the other side of the wood,' said Little Red Riding-Hood.

'What do you do when you get there, my dear?' said the wolf.

'I knock at the door.'

'And what does your granny do then?'

'She says: "Who is there?"'

'And what do you do next, my dear?'

'I say: "It's Little Red Riding-Hood, Granny, and I have brought you some cakes and cream and eggs and a little pot of butter."'

'And what does Granny do next, my dear?'

'She calls out: "Pull the bobbin and the latch will go up."'

When the Wolf heard this he ran as fast as he could to Little Red Riding-Hood's granny's cottage by the quickest way.

But Little Red Riding-Hood did not do as her mother had told her. She played on the way and amused herself by picking wild flowers and watching the birds and chasing after the butterflies, so she went very slowly through the wood.

The wolf soon arrived at the grandmother's cottage and knocked at the door, *rat-tat-tat*.

'Who is there?' called the grandmother.

'Oh, it's Little Red Riding-Hood,' said the wolf, making his voice as like the little girl's as he could. 'I've brought you some cakes and cream and eggs and a little pot of butter.'

Then the good old woman, who was ill in bed, called out:

'Pull the bobbin, my dear, and the latch will go up.'

The wolf pulled the bobbin; the latch went up and the door opened. At once he sprang on the poor old grandmother and gobbled her up in an instant, for he was very hungry; but her nightcap fell on the floor.

Then he went over and shut the door again. Next he put on the grandmother's spectacles and nightcap, trying to hide his face, but he could not hide his ears. Then he got into bed to wait for Little Red Riding-Hood.

He had not long to wait.

Soon the little girl knocked at the door, *rat-tat-tat*.

'Who is there?' said the wolf, making his voice as like the grandmother's as he could.

Little Red Riding-Hood thought that her granny's voice sounded very hoarse and rough but she supposed that Granny must have a bad cold. So she said:

'It's Little Red Riding-Hood, Granny, and I've brought you some cakes and cream and eggs and a little pot of butter.'

'Pull the bobbin and the latch will go up,' called the wolf.

So Little Red Riding-Hood pulled the bobbin, the latch went up and the door opened.

She went inside and walked over to the bed to see her granny, but the cunning wolf had pulled up the bedclothes

so she could not see him very well.

Then he said: 'Shut the door, and come and sit close beside me, my dear.'

So Little Red Riding-Hood shut the door and sat down on a stool close beside the wolf in the bed. She thought how strange her grandmother looked today, so she said:

'Granny, what big arms you've got!'

'All the better to hug you with, my dear.'

'Granny, what big ears you've got!'

'All the better to hear you with, my dear.'

'Granny, what big eyes you've got!'

'All the better to see you with, my dear.'

'Granny, what big teeth you've got!'

'All the better to EAT you with.'

And as he said that, the wicked wolf jumped up in bed to spring on Little Red Riding-Hood and gobble her up.

But just at that moment the door opened and in ran a woodcutter. He was Little Red Riding-Hood's father, and he had seen his little girl go into her grandmother's cottage and had come to take her home.

He was horrified to see a wolf, dressed in Granny's nightcap and spectacles, just about to swallow Little Red Riding-Hood up. But he quickly leapt forward and struck the wicked wolf a fierce blow with his axe – and that was the end of him. Then he picked up poor Little Red Riding-Hood in his arms, and carried her safely home.

RAIN AND SHINE

Here we go round the mulberry bush,
The mulberry bush, the mulberry bush,
Here we go round the mulberry bush,
On a cold and frosty morning.

This is the way we wash our hands,
Wash our hands, wash our hands,
This is the way we wash our hands,
On a cold and frosty morning.

This is the way we wash our clothes,
Wash our clothes, wash our clothes,
This is the way we wash our clothes,
On a cold and frosty morning.

This is the way we go to school,
Go to school, go to school,
This is the way we go to school,
On a cold and frosty morning.

This is the way we come out of school,
Come out of school, come out of school,
This is the way we come out of school,
On a cold and frosty morning.

Doctor Foster went to Gloucester
In a shower of rain;
He stepped in a puddle,
Right up to his middle,
And never went there again.

The north wind doth blow,
And we shall have snow,
And what will poor Robin do then,
Poor thing?

He'll sit in a barn,
And keep himself warm,
And hide his head under his wing,
Poor thing.

It's raining, it's pouring,
The old man's snoring;
He got into bed
And bumped his head
And couldn't get up in the morning.

Rain, rain, go away,
Come again another day,
Little Johnny wants to play.

Rain, rain, go to Spain,
Never show your face again.

Daffy-down-dilly
is new come to town,
With a yellow petticoat,
and a green gown.

March winds and April showers

Bring forth May flowers.

Ipsey Wipsey spider climbing up the spout; Down came the rain and washed the spider out; Out came the sunshine and dried up all the rain; Ipsey Wipsey spider climbing up again.

JACK AND THE BEANSTALK

There was once a poor widow who lived in a little cottage in the country with her son Jack. Jack was a good son, though sometimes lazy and thoughtless, but they grew poorer and poorer until at last all they had left was one cow.

'I have no more money to buy bread,' said Jack's mother sadly. 'You must take my poor cow to market and sell her, or we shall starve. Be sure to get a good price for her.'

So Jack set off for market with the cow. On the way he met an old man who pulled out of his pocket some strange-looking beans, purple and black and red.

'What pretty beans!' cried Jack.

'They are wonderful beans,' said the old man, 'and worth a fortune, but you shall have them in exchange for your cow if you like.'

'Yes I will,' said Jack, and the next moment he found himself alone in the road with no cow and only some beans in his pocket.

His mother was waiting anxiously for him when he got home, and when she heard his story she was very angry.

She threw the beans into the garden and she and Jack had to go hungry to bed.

Next morning Jack woke to find that the sun could not shine in through his window. The light was pale green, and outside were the green leaves and scarlet flowers of a strange large plant. He ran into the garden, and found that the beans had taken root in the night and had grown into a great plant so tall that its top was out of sight in the clouds. The thick stalks of this bean-plant had twisted round each other so that they made a kind of ladder.

'I wonder where it ends,' said Jack. 'I must go up that ladder and see,' and he began to climb. Up and up he went. He grew tired and he was very hungry,

but he rested for a while and then went on bravely. After hours had passed and he was up above the clouds, he came to a strange country and sat down on a stone to rest.

Suddenly a woman appeared. 'In a castle not far from here,' she said, 'lives a giant who killed your father and stole all his treasures. You must get them back, especially the hen that lays golden eggs and the harp that talks, and so repay all your mother's kindness to you.'

As she stopped speaking she vanished, and Jack knew she must be a fairy. He went on his way, and at sunset reached a great castle. In the doorway was standing an enormously tall giantess.

'Please will you give me something to eat?' asked Jack.

'Don't you know that my husband is a giant who eats boys when he catches them?' replied the giantess. 'But if you like, you may come in and help me when he is out, and I shall hide you when he comes home.'

Jack was afraid but he knew he must obey the fairy and try to get back the treasures the giant had stolen, so he agreed to help her.

So the giantess took Jack in and gave him something to eat and drink.

By and by the house began to shake.

'My husband is coming!' cried the giantess, and she quickly hid Jack in the oven.

Then the giant came in sniffing, and roared in a voice like thunder:

'FEE-FI-FO-FUM,

I SMELL THE BLOOD OF AN ENGLISHMAN!

BE HE ALIVE OR BE HE DEAD, I'LL GRIND HIS BONES TO MAKE MY BREAD.'

'Nonsense!' cried his wife. 'It's only the sheep I killed this morning.' And she put on the table a pie so

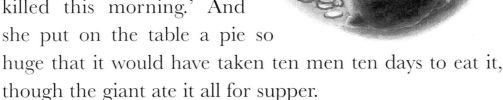

huge that it would have taken ten men ten days to eat it, though the giant ate it all for supper.

When he had finished his meal, the giant told his wife to bring him his money-bags. Two bags were brought, one full of gold and the other full of silver, and the giant counted the money until he fell asleep.

His wife was busy in the kitchen, and so Jack crept out of the oven, seized the money-bags, and ran off to the top of the beanstalk. He climbed down it as fast as he could, and soon was safe in his mother's garden.

His mother was overjoyed to see him, and Jack told her all about his adventures, and gave her the bags of gold and silver. Now they were able to live much more comfortably.

But it was not long until Jack felt he must climb the beanstalk again, to get back some more of his father's treasures which the giant had stolen. So he climbed to the top of the beanstalk and arrived once more at the giant's

castle. He had dyed his face and hair brown so that the giantess would not know him; but it was some time before she would take him in, so angry was she with the boy who had taken the giant's money-bags. At last she let him into the castle to help with the work as before, and gave him some food.

By and by the house began to shake.

'My husband is coming!' cried the giantess, and she quickly hid Jack in the cupboard.

Then the giant came in, sniffing. He looked around the kitchen and roared:

'FEE-FI-FO-FUM,

I SMELL THE BLOOD OF AN ENGLISHMAN!

BE HE ALIVE OR BE HE DEAD

I'LL GRIND HIS BONES TO MAKE MY BREAD.'

'Nonsense,' replied his wife. 'It's only the pig I killed this morning.'

After eating the whole pig the giant called for his magic

hen, and a wonderful hen with feathers of crimson and gold was put before him. The giant said to the hen, 'LAY!' And at once it laid a golden egg.

Soon afterwards the giant fell asleep, and then Jack came out of the cupboard, tucked the hen under his arm, and ran off to the top of the beanstalk. He climbed down it and brought the hen safely home to his mother. As they could now have a golden egg every day, they were soon very rich.

But before long Jack felt he must go back to the giant's castle and try to get the magic harp the fairy had spoken about. This time he dyed his hair red, and off he went up the beanstalk once more to the giant's castle. He did not dare to ask the giantess to let him in again, but slipped inside when she was not looking.

By and by the house began to shake.

Jack looked round for a different place to hide, and climbed safely into the copper.

The giant came in, sniffing. 'I smell fresh meat!' he roared.

'FEE-FI-FO-FUM,
I SMELL THE BLOOD OF AN ENGLISHMAN!
BE HE ALIVE OR BE HE DEAD
I'LL GRIND HIS BONES TO MAKE MY BREAD.'

'Nonsense,' replied his wife. 'It's only the calf I killed this morning.'

But the giant did not believe her, and so he searched every corner of the kitchen. He even put his hand on the

lid of the copper, and Jack trembled with fear, but he did not lift the lid. At last he sat down and ate an enormous supper. After it he called for his harp.

A wonderful golden harp was brought. The giant said, 'PLAY!' And it played beautiful music until he fell asleep.

Then Jack crept out of the copper, seized the harp and ran off. But the harp was enchanted and it cried out: 'Master! Master!'

The giant awoke and ran after Jack, roaring with fury, but he had eaten so much that he could not run as fast as usual.

So Jack reached the beanstalk first and hurried down it. The giant was astonished to see the beanstalk stretching away beneath him, but he began to climb down it at once. Jack felt the beanstalk begin to shake, and when he got to the bottom he could see the giant's legs showing through the clouds and coming down fast after him.

Jack shouted to his mother to bring him an axe, and at once he cut the beanstalk through. Down came the beanstalk and down crashed the giant, making a great deep hole in the ground where he hit it, and that was the end of him.

Jack showed his mother the magic harp and asked her to forgive him for having been so lazy and unhelpful. Of course his mother forgave him, and with the harp, the golden eggs, and the gold and silver they lived in happiness and comfort ever after.

Hop, Skip and Jump

If all the world was paper,
And all the sea was ink,
If all the trees were bread and cheese,
What should we have to drink?

A man in the wilderness asked me,

How many strawberries grow in the sea?

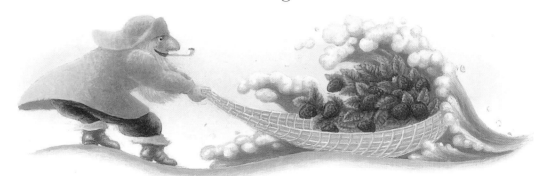

I answered him, as I thought good,

As many red herrings as swim in the wood.

See-saw, Margery Daw,
Jacky shall have a new master;
Jacky shall have but a penny a day,
Because he can't work any faster.

Ring-a-ring o' roses,
A pocket full of posies,
A-TISHOO! A-TISHOO!
We all fall down.

The cows are in the meadow
Lying fast asleep,
A-TISHOO! A-TISHOO!
We all get up again.

London Bridge is falling down,
Falling down, falling down,
London Bridge is falling down,
My fair lady.

Build it up with wood and clay,
Wood and clay, wood and clay,
Build it up with wood and clay,
My fair lady.

Wood and clay will wash away,
Wash away, wash away,
Wood and clay will wash away,
My fair lady.

Build it up with bricks and mortar,
Bricks and mortar, bricks and mortar,
Build it up with bricks and mortar,
My fair lady.

Bricks and mortar will not stay,
Will not stay, will not stay,
Bricks and mortar will not stay,
My fair lady.

Build it up with iron and steel,
Iron and steel, iron and steel,
Build it up with iron and steel,
My fair lady.

Iron and steel will bend and bow,
Bend and bow, bend and bow,
Iron and steel will bend and bow,
My fair lady.

Build it up with silver and gold,
Silver and gold, silver and gold,
Build it up with silver and gold,
My fair lady.

Silver and gold will be stolen away,
Stolen away, stolen away,
Silver and gold will be stolen away,
My fair lady.

Set a man to watch all night,
Watch all night, watch all night,
Sct a man to watch all night,
My fair lady.

Suppose the man should fall asleep,
Fall asleep, fall asleep,
Suppose the man should fall asleep,
My fair lady.

Give him a pipe to smoke all night,
Smoke all night, smoke all night,
Give him a pipe to smoke all night,
My fair lady.

I saw a peacock with a fiery tail
I saw a blazing comet drop down hail
I saw a cloud with ivy curled around
I saw a sturdy oak creep on the ground
I saw an ant swallow up a whale
I saw a raging sea brim full of ale
I saw a Venice glass sixteen foot deep
I saw a well full of men's tears that weep
I saw their eyes all in a flame of fire
I saw a house high as the moon and higher
I saw the sun at twelve o'clock at night
I saw the man who saw this wondrous sight.

Little Nancy Etticoat,
With a white petticoat,
And a red nose;
She has no feet or hands,
The longer she stands
The shorter she grows.

Peter Piper picked a peck
of pickled pepper;
A peck of pickled pepper
Peter Piper picked.
If Peter Piper picked a peck
of pickled pepper,
Where's the peck of pickled pepper
Peter Piper picked?

She sells sea-shells
on the sea shore;
The shells that she sells
are sea-shells I'm sure.
So if she sells sea-shells
on the sea shore,
I'm sure that the shells
are sea-shore shells.

PUSS IN BOOTS

Once upon a time there was a miller who had three sons. The miller was quite poor, and when he died he had only three things to leave – his mill, his ass, and his cat. He left them all to his sons. The eldest son had the mill, the second son had the ass, and the youngest son had the cat.

The youngest son was very disappointed. 'My brothers can make a living by working together,' he said, 'for one can grind corn and the other can carry it to market in sacks on the ass. I have nothing but a cat, and I shall soon die of hunger.'

But the cat heard and rubbed against his master's legs and said: 'Don't be down-hearted, master. Just buy me a pair of boots and a bag and you will soon see that you have not been as poorly treated as you think. I am far more valuable than the mill or the ass.'

The cat's master agreed to do this, and spent his last coins on a splendid pair of boots and a strong bag for the cat.

Puss was full of joy and pride as he put on the fine boots. 'Now I am Puss in Boots,' he cried, and taking the bag he put some bran and lettuce into it. Then he went into a field where there were a great number of rabbits, and stretched himself out as if he were dead, with the strings of the bag between his paws. He waited until some young rabbit, who knew nothing of the tricks of the world, should come into the bag to eat the bran and lettuce.

Almost at once he got what he wanted. A foolish young rabbit jumped into the bag and at once the cat pulled the strings tight and caught it.

Delighted at his luck, Puss set off for the palace, and there he asked to see the king. The servants were astonished to see a cat with boots on, but they did as he asked and brought him to the king's throne.

Bowing low to the king, the cat said: 'Your Majesty, my master, the Marquis of Carabas, sends you this rabbit as a present.'

'Tell your master,' said the king, 'that I thank him very much for his kind present, which I am pleased to accept.'

Next day, the cat hid himself in a cornfield, and caught two pigeons in his bag. Again he went to the palace, and there he presented the birds to the king, saying they were from his master, the Marquis of Carabas. (This was the title by which he had chosen to call his master.)

The king was pleased with the pigeons, and ordered some money to be given to the cat. After this for several weeks, Puss took the king presents of game his master was supposed to have caught, and the king graciously accepted them.

Now the king had a very beautiful daughter, who was his only child. One day Puss, who had seen the princess, and thought her the most beautiful girl in the world, heard that the king was to drive with the princess along the road by the river.

He went to his master and said: 'Master, if you will do as I ask, your fortune is made. All you have to do is to bathe in the river at the place I shall show you, and leave the rest to me.'

His master did as the cat had asked him, and as soon as he was in the water, Puss hid his worn and faded clothes.

Soon afterwards the king's coach drew near, and then the cat began to shout: 'Help! Help! My master, the Marquis of Carabas, is drowning!'

Hearing the cries, the king put his head out of the carriage window, and recognizing the cat who had so often brought him presents, he ordered the guards to make haste and rescue the Marquis of Carabas.

While they were pulling the poor Marquis out of the river, Puss explained to the king that while his master was bathing, some thieves had come and stolen his clothes. So, though his master was saved, he had no clothes to put on.

The king at once ordered a magnificent suit of clothes to be brought for the Marquis of Carabas, and when the miller's son was brought to the door of the coach to pay his respects to the king and the princess, he looked so handsome in his fine clothes that the princess fell in love with him at once, and the king invited him into the coach beside them.

Puss, delighted at the success of his plans, ran on in front, and seeing some men at work in the fields, said to

them: 'My good people, if you do not tell the king, who is coming this way, that these fields belong to the Marquis of Carabas, you will be chopped into mincemeat.'

The men were much alarmed, and when the king passed by and asked them who owned the fields, they replied: 'They belong to the Marquis of Carabas.'

'You have a fine estate,' said the king to the miller's son.

The young man could only bow and blush, for he was too astonished to reply.

The cat, who still ran on in front of the coach, kept telling the same story to everyone he met, and they all told the king that the land on which they were working belonged to the Marquis of Carabas, for they were afraid that they would be chopped into mincemeat. And so the king was greatly surprised at the riches of the Marquis of Carabas.

At last Puss reached a great castle where lived an ogre who was also a magician. This ogre was the richest person in the land, for all the country round about, through which the king had passed on his drive, belonged to him.

Puss asked permission to pay his respects to the ogre and was taken into his presence.

'I have been told that you are a great magician,' he said, 'and that you can change yourself into any shape you like! Is this true?'

'Indeed it is,' said the ogre, changing himself into a lion, which roared at the cat.

Puss was much alarmed and, springing out of the

window, scrambled up a water-pipe – a most difficult thing to do in his boots. Not till the ogre had returned to his own shape would he come down again.

'You are wonderfully clever,' he said to the ogre, 'but I suppose you can only turn yourself into great and strong creatures like yourself. You will not be able to take the shape of a small creature such as a mouse.'

'Oh yes I can,' replied the ogre. 'You will soon see.' And he changed himself into a mouse and ran across the floor.

Puss no sooner saw the mouse than he sprang upon it, and ate it up before it had time to turn into an ogre again.

Then he hurried to meet the king, for he had heard the coach entering the courtyard. 'Welcome, Your Majesty, to the castle of the Marquis of Carabas!' said he.

'What, my Lord Marquis,' cried the king, 'so this great castle is yours also! Let us see the inside, I pray you.'

So the miller's son gave his arm to the princess, and they all entered the castle, where they found a fine banquet which the ogre had given orders to have ready for his friends.

The king was highly delighted with the feast, the splendid castle, and the good manners of the handsome young Marquis, and so was his daughter.

'My Lord,' said the king, 'I offer you the honour of my daughter's hand in marriage.'

The young man accepted the honour with joy, and he

and the princess were married that very day. They lived together in happiness for many years, and when the king died, they became king and queen.

The cat became a great lord, and never needed to hunt mice and rats again, except for fun.

ONE, TWO, THREE

He that would thrive
Must rise at five;
He that hath thriven
May lie till seven;
He that will never thrive
May lie till eleven.

One, two, three, four, five,
Once I caught a fish alive,

Six, seven, eight, nine, ten,
Then I let it go again.

Why did you let it go?
Because it bit my finger so.

Which finger did it bite?
The little finger on the right.

One
for sorrow,

Two
for joy,

Three
for a girl,

Four
for a boy,

Five
for silver,

Six
for gold,

Seven
for a secret
ne'er to be told.

Baa, baa,
black sheep,
Have you any wool?
Yes, sir, yes, sir,
Three bags full;
One for the master,
And one for the dame,
And one for the little boy
Who lives down the lane.

Rub-a-dub-dub, three men in a tub,

And who do you think they be?

The butcher, the baker, the candlestick-maker;

Turn 'em out, knaves all three!

Monday's child is fair of face,
Tuesday's child is full of grace,
Wednesday's child is full of woe,
Thursday's child has far to go,
Friday's child is loving and giving,
Saturday's child works hard for its living,
But the child that's born on the Sabbath day
Is bonny and blithe, and good and gay.

Thirty days hath September,
April, June, and November;
All the rest have thirty-one,
Excepting February alone,
And that has twenty-eight days clear
And twenty-nine in each leap year.

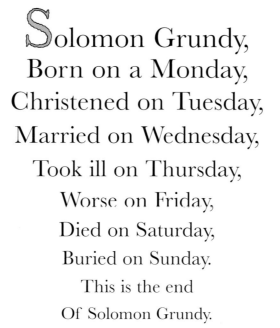

Solomon Grundy,
Born on a Monday,
Christened on Tuesday,
Married on Wednesday,
Took ill on Thursday,
Worse on Friday,
Died on Saturday,
Buried on Sunday.
This is the end
Of Solomon Grundy.

THE THREE BILLY GOATS GRUFF

Three goats once lived together in a field. The littlest one was called Little Billy Goat Gruff. The next one was bigger than Little Billy Goat Gruff so he was called Big Billy Goat Gruff. But the third one was the biggest of them all and so he was called Great Big Billy Goat Gruff.

At the end of their field was a river, and across the river was another field. Now this field was empty and the grass there grew rich and long and very green. Little Billy Goat Gruff said he could see some beautiful rosy apples on a tree over there. Big Billy Goat Gruff said there was plenty of lovely clover in that field. And Great Big Billy Goat Gruff said he had seen ripe red berries growing there as well. They all longed to cross over the river.

Now there was a low plank bridge across the river, but under it there lived a horrible troll who liked to eat goats better than anything else. So the three Billy Goats never dared to cross the bridge into that lovely empty field in case the troll caught them.

One day Little Billy Goat Gruff was specially hungry and he told his brothers: 'I'm going to go over and have

some of those rosy apples to eat.

His brothers said, 'Be careful; remember the troll. He'll get you.' But off went Little Billy Goat Gruff, trit trot trit trot over the bridge.

'I'm too small for him,' he said.

But when he was halfway across, the troll suddenly put his head out and said, 'Who's running over *my* bridge?'

'It's only Little Billy Goat Gruff.'

'I'm going to eat you up,' said the troll.

But Little Billy Goat Gruff said, 'Don't eat me because I'm only Little Billy Goat Gruff. I've got a brother called Big Billy Goat Gruff, who is much bigger and fatter than I am. Why don't you wait for him?'

'All right, I will,' said the troll. 'You may go across.'

So Little Billy Goat Gruff trotted across the bridge to the other side and began to feast on the rich green grass and the beautiful rosy apples.

When Big Billy Goat Gruff saw that Little Billy Goat Gruff had got safely across, off he went, trit trot trit trot, over the bridge too.

When he was halfway across the troll put his head out and said, 'Who's running over *my* bridge.'

'It's only Big Billy Goat Gruff.'

'Then I'm going to eat you up,' said the troll. 'Your brother said you were coming.'

But Big Billy Goat Gruff said, 'Don't eat me, because

I'm only Big Billy Goat Gruff. I've got a brother called Great Big Billy Goat Gruff, who is still bigger and fatter than I am. Why don't you wait for him?'

'All right, I will,' said the troll. 'You may go across.'

So Big Billy Goat Gruff trotted across the bridge to the other side and began to feast on the rich green grass with Little Billy Goat Gruff and to enjoy the lovely clover too.

Then Great Big Billy Goat Gruff thought it was time he went over to join his brothers and have some of the rich green grass and the ripe red berries. So off he went, trit trot trit trot, over the bridge. When he was halfway across the troll put his head out and said, 'Who's running over *my* bridge?'

'It's Great Big Billy Goat Gruff.'

'You're the one I'm going to eat up,' said the troll. 'Your

brother said you were coming, and I've been waiting for you.'

But trying not to look frightened, Great Big Billy Goat Gruff said, 'Oh, are you? Come and try.'

Then the troll jumped up on to the bridge, but Great Big Billy Goat Gruff put down his head, ran at the troll and knocked him off the bridge with his horns so that he disappeared under the water of the river.

And Great Big Billy Goat Gruff trotted across the bridge to the other side and joined Big Billy Goat Gruff and Little Billy Goat Gruff in the empty field. And they all enjoyed the rich green grass. Great Big Billy Goat Gruff ate the ripe red berries, Big Billy Goat Gruff ate the lovely clover and Little Billy Goat Gruff ate the beautiful rosy apples. And they all grew very fat.

CAT AND MOUSE

Hickory, dickory, dock,

The mouse ran up the clock.

The clock struck one,

The mouse ran down,

Hickory, dickory, dock.

The winds they did blow,
The leaves they did wag;
Along came a beggar boy,
And put me in his bag.

He took me up to London,
A lady did me buy,
Put me in a golden cage,
And hung me up on high.

With apples by the fire,
And nuts for to crack,
Besides a little feather bed
To rest my little back.

There was a crooked man,
　　And he walked a crooked mile,
He found a crooked sixpence
　　Against a crooked stile;
He bought a crooked cat,
　　Which caught a crooked mouse,
And they all lived together
　　In a little crooked house.

Three blind mice,
See how they run!
They all ran after the farmer's wife;
Who cut off their tails with a carving knife,
Did you ever see such a thing in your life,
As three blind mice?

Hoddley, poddley,
puddle and frogs,
Cats are to marry
the poodle dogs;
Cats in blue jackets
and dogs in red hats,
What will become
of the mice and the rats?

Six little mice sat down to spin;
Pussy passed by and she peeped in.
What are you doing, my little men?
Weaving coats for gentlemen.

Shall I come in and cut off your threads?
No, no, Mistress Pussy, you'd bite off our heads.
Oh, no, I'll not; I'll help you to spin.
That may be so, but you don't come in.

Three little kittens
They lost their mittens,
And they began to cry,
Oh, Mother dear,
We sadly fear
Our mittens we have lost
What! lost your mittens,
You naughty kittens!
Then you shall have no pie.
Mee-ow, mee-ow, mee-ow.
No, you shall have no pie.

The three little kittens
They found their mittens,
And they began to cry,
Oh, Mother dear,
See here, see here,
Our mittens we have found.
Put on your mittens,
You silly kittens,
And you shall have some pie.
Purr-r, purr-r, purr-r,
Oh let us have some pie.

The three little kittens
Put on their mittens
And soon ate up the pie;
Oh, Mother dear,
We greatly fear
Our mittens we have soiled
What! soiled your mittens,
You naughty kittens!
Then they began to sigh,
Mee-ow, mee-ow, mee-ow,
Then they began to sigh.

The three little kittens
They washed their mittens,
And hung them out to dry;
Oh, Mother dear,
Do you not hear,
Our mittens we have washed.
What! washed your mittens,
Then you're good kittens,
But I smell a rat close by.
Mee-ow, mee-ow, mee-ow,
We smell a rat close by.

Ding, dong, bell, Pussy's in the well.
Who put her in? Little Johnny Green.
Who pulled her out? Little Tommy Stout.
What a naughty boy was that
To try to drown poor pussy cat,
Who never did him any harm,
And killed the mice in his father's barn.

Hark, hark,
The dogs do bark,
The beggars are
coming to town;
Some in rags,
And some in jags,
And one in a velvet gown.

Three young rats with black felt hats,
Three young ducks with white straw flats,
Three young dogs with curling tails,
Three young cats with demi-veils,
Went out to walk with three young pigs
In satin vests and sorrel wigs;
But suddenly it chanced to rain
And so they all went home again.

Pussy cat, pussy cat, where have you been?
I've been to London to look at the queen.
Pussy cat, pussy cat, what did you there?
I frightened a little mouse under her chair.

THE THREE LITTLE PIGS

Once upon a time there were three little pigs. Their mother was too poor to keep them all at home, so as soon as they were big enough she sent them out into the world to seek their fortunes.

The first little pig said goodbye to his brothers and set off alone. Soon he met a man carrying a truss of straw. The little pig asked the man politely to give him the straw. So the man gave him the truss of straw and the little pig built a house with it.

By and by a wolf came along and saw the house and smelt the pig inside. He knocked at the door and said: 'Little Pig, Little Pig, let me come in.'

But the pig knew the wolf's voice, so he replied:

'No, no, by the hair of my chinny-chin-chin.'

'Then,' said the wolf, 'I'll huff and I'll puff, and I'll blow your house in.' So he huffed and he puffed till he blew the house in, and then he ate up the first little pig.

The second little pig said goodbye to his brother and set off alone. Soon he met a man carrying a bundle of sticks. The little pig asked the man politely to give him the sticks. So the man gave him the bundle of sticks and the

little pig built a house with it.

By and by the wolf came along, and saw the house and smelt the pig inside. He knocked at the door and said: 'Little Pig, Little Pig, let me come in.'

But the pig peeped out and saw the wolf's ears through the keyhole, so he replied:

'No, no, by the hair on my chinny-chin-chin.'

'Then,' said the wolf, 'I'll huff and I'll puff, and I'll blow your house in.' So he huffed and he puffed, and he huffed and he puffed, till he blew the house in, and then he ate up the second little pig.

The third little pig went along alone and met a man carrying a load of bricks. The little pig asked the man politely to give him the bricks. So the man gave him the load of bricks and the little pig built a house with them. By and by the wolf came along and saw the house and smelt

the pig inside. He knocked at the door and said, 'Little Pig, Little Pig, let me come in.'

But the pig peeped out and saw the wolf's paws under the door, so he replied:

'No, no, by the hair on my chinny-chin-chin.'

'Then,' said the wolf, 'I'll huff and I'll puff, and I'll blow your house in.' So he huffed and he puffed, and he huffed and he puffed, and he huffed and he puffed, but he couldn't blow the house in. And when he saw that he couldn't blow the house in no matter how hard he huffed and he puffed, he said: 'Little Pig, Little Pig, I can tell you where there are some nice turnips.'

'Where?' asked the little pig.

'In the field at the top of the lane,' said the wolf. 'If you will be ready at six o'clock tomorrow morning, we'll go and get some together for dinner.'

'Yes, I'll be ready,' said the little pig.

But next morning the little pig got up at five o'clock, and ran to the field and got the turnips before the wolf came.

At six o'clock the wolf came and said:

'Little Pig, are you ready?'

'Ready!' said the little pig. 'I've been and come back, and I've plenty of turnips for my dinner.'

The wolf was very angry, but he said smoothly: 'Little Pig, Little Pig, I know where there are some nice apples.'

'Where?' asked the little pig.

'On a tree at the end of the lane. If you will be ready

at five o'clock tomorrow we'll get some together.'

'Yes, I'll be ready,' said the little pig.

But next morning the little pig got up at four o'clock and ran to the end of the lane and climbed the apple tree.

He picked a lot of apples but just when he was climbing down he saw the wolf coming. He was very frightened, so he stayed where he was, up the tree. When the wolf came to the tree he said:

'Little Pig, why didn't you wait for me? Are they nice apples?'

'Yes, very nice,' said the little pig. 'Let me throw you one down to taste.' And he threw an apple so far that while the wolf was going to pick it up, the little pig had time to jump down and run home.

Next day the wolf came again to the little pig's house and knocked at the door and said:

'Little Pig, Little Pig, there is a fair this afternoon. Will you come with me at three o'clock?'

'Yes, I'll be ready,' said the little pig.

But the little pig started again before the wolf came, and went to the fair. There he bought a butter-churn. He was carrying it home when he saw the wolf coming. The little pig was very frightened, so he got into the churn to hide. But as he got in, the churn fell over and began to roll over and over downhill with the little pig inside. The wolf saw a strange round thing rolling towards him and he was so frightened by it that he ran away home without going to the fair.

At the bottom of the hill the little pig got out of the churn and went into his house. By and by the wolf came again to the little pig's house and knocked at the door and said:

'Little Pig, I couldn't come to the fair because a big round thing ran after me right down the hill.'

'Aha!' said the little pig. 'I frightened you then! That was only my butter-churn which I bought at the fair, and I was inside it.'

Then the wolf was very angry, and said: 'I'm going to get up on the roof and climb down the chimney and eat you up.'

So he began to climb on to the roof. But the little pig poked up the fire and hung a large pot full of water over it. Just when he heard the noise of the wolf coming down the chimney he lifted the lid of the pot, and in fell the wolf. The little pig put on the lid, boiled him and ate him for supper. And he lived happily afterwards in his house of bricks.

STAR LIGHT,
STAR BRIGHT

Go to bed late,

Stay very small;

Go to bed early,

Grow very tall.

Wee Willie Winkie runs through the town,
Upstairs and downstairs in his nightgown.
Rapping at the window, crying at the lock,
Are the children all in bed, for now it's eight o'clock?

Come, let's to bed,
Says Sleepy-head.
Tarry a while, says Slow.
Put on the pan,
Says Greedy Nan,
We'll sup before we go.

Diddle, diddle, dumpling,
my son JOHN,
Went to bed with
his trousers ON;
One shoe OFF,
and one shoe ON,
Diddle, diddle, dumpling,
my son JOHN.

Goosey, goosey gander,
Wither shall I wander?
Upstairs and downstairs
And in my
lady's chamber.

There I met an old man
Who would not say his prayers,
I took him by the left leg
And threw him down the stairs.

Little Boy Blue,
    Come blow your horn,
The sheep's in the meadow,
    The cow's in the corn.
Where is the boy
    Who looks after the sheep?

He's under a haystack
    Fast asleep.
Will you wake him?
    No, not I,
For if I do,
    He's sure to cry.

Hush-a-bye, baby, on the tree top,

When the wind blows the cradle will rock;

When the bough breaks the cradle will fall,

Down will come baby, cradle, and all.

There was an old woman tossed up in a basket,
Seventeen times as high as the moon;
Where she was going I couldn't but ask it,
For in her hand she carried a broom.

Old woman, old woman, old woman, quoth I,
Where are you going to up so high?
To brush the cobwebs off the sky!
May I go with you? Aye, by and by.

Hush, little baby, don't say a word,
Papa's going to buy you a mocking bird.

If the mocking bird won't sing,
Papa's going to buy you a diamond ring.

If the diamond ring turns to brass,
Papa's going to buy you a looking-glass

If the looking-glass gets broke,
Papa's going to buy you a billy goat.

If that billy goat runs away,
Papa's going to buy you another today.

Star light, star bright,

First star I see tonight,

I wish I may, I wish I might,

Have the wish I wish tonight.

Boys and girls come out to play,
The moon doth shine as bright as day.
Leave your supper and leave your sleep,
And join your playfellows in the street.
Come with a whoop and come with a call,
Come with a good will or not at all.
Up the ladder and down the wall,
A half-penny loaf will serve us all;
You find milk, and I'll find flour,
And we'll have a pudding in half an hour.

INDEX OF FIRST LINES

A farmer went trotting upon his grey mare	47
A man in the wilderness asked me	95
A wise old	53
Baa, baa	117
Bobby Shaftoe's gone to sea	66
Boys and girls come out to play	155
Bull's eyes and targets	16
Christmas is coming	31
Come, let's to bed	148
Cross-patch	29
Curly locks, Curly locks	65
Daffy-down-dilly	84
Diddle, diddle, dumpling	148
Ding, dong, bell, Pussy's in the well	136
Doctor Foster went to Gloucester	80
Georgie Porgie	60
Goosey, goosey gander	149
Go to bed late	146
Hark, Hark	137
Hector Protector	8
Here we go round the mulberry bush	78
He that would thrive	114
Hey diddle, diddle	51
Hickety, Pickety	46
Hickory, dickory, dock	128
Hoddley, poddley	132

Humpty Dumpty sat on a wall 12

Hush-a-bye, baby, on the tree top 151

Hush, little baby, don't say a word 153

If all the world was paper 94

I had a little nut tree 37

I'm the king of the castle 9

Ipsey Wipsey spider 85

I saw a peacock with a fiery tail 102

It's raining, it's pouring 82

Jack 36

Jack and Jill 71

Jenny Wren fell sick 52

Lavender's blue 61

Little Bo-peep has lost her sheep 44

Little Boy Blue 150

Little Jack Horner 32

Little Miss Muffet 30

Little Nancy Etticoat 103

Little Polly Flinders sat among the cinders 70

London Bridge is falling down 98

Magpie, magpie, flutter and flee 46

March winds and April showers 84

Mary had a little lamb 48

Mary, Mary, quite contrary 62

Monday's child is fair of face 119

Oh, the grand old 15

Old King Cole 10

Old Mother Hubbard 26

One 116

One, two, three, four, five   115
Pease porridge hot   27
Peter Piper picked a peck   104
Polly put the kettle on   33
Pussy cat, pussy cat, where have you been?   139
Rain, rain, go away   83
Ride a cock-horse   49
Ring-a-ring o' roses   97
Roses are red   64
Rub-a-dub-dub, three men in a tub   118
Sally go round the sun   67
See-saw, Margery Daw   96
She sells sea-shells   105
Simple Simon met a pieman   34
Sing a song of sixpence   19
Six little mice sat down to spin   133
Solomon Grundy   121
Star light, star bright   154
The lion and the unicorn   11
The north wind doth blow   81
The Queen of Hearts   13
There was a crooked man   130
There was a little   64
There was an old woman   28
There was an old woman tossed up in a basket   152
The winds they did blow   129
Thirty days hath September   120
Three blind mice   131
Three little kittens   134

Three young rats with black felt hats   138

Tom, Tom   67

Tweedledum and Tweedledee   14

Wee Willie Winkie runs through the town   147

What are little boys   63

Where are you going to, my pretty maid?   68

Yankee Doodle came to town   50